D1274586

Ancient Greek
CULTURE

Henry Bensinger

Published in 2014 by The Rosen Publishing Group, Inc.
29 East 21st Street, New York, NY 10010

First Edition

Editor: Joanne Randolph
Book Design: Kate Vlachos

Photo Credits: Cover Michele Falzone/Photographer's Choice RF/Getty Images; p. 5 Markus Gann/Shutterstock.com; p. 6 iStockphoto/Thinkstock; p. 7 Hemera Technologies/ AbleStock.com/Thinkstock; p. 8 Photolibrary/Dave Porter Peterborough Uk/Getty Images; p. 9 Wayne Walton/Lonely Planet Images/Getty Images; p. 11 Rechitan Sorin/Shutterstock. com; pp. 13, 22 Panos Karas/Shutterstock.com; p. 14 © iStockphoto.com/Duncan Walker; p. 15 DEA/G. Dagli Orti/De Agostini Picture Library/Getty Images; p. 16 The Bridgeman Art Library/French School/Getty Images; p. 17 Photos.com/Thinkstock; p. 18 Ekaterina Pokrovsky/Shutterstock.com; p. 19 Gjon Mili/Time & Life Pictures/Getty Images; p. 20 DEA/M. Carrieri/De Agostini/Getty Images; p. 21 Hisham Ibrahim/Photographer's Choice RF/Getty Images.

Library of Congress Cataloging-in-Publication Data

Bensinger, Henry.
  Ancient Greek culture / by Henry Bensinger. — First edition.
    pages cm. — (Spotlight on ancient civilizations: Greece)
  Includes index.
  ISBN 978-1-4777-0769-2 (library binding) — ISBN 978-1-4777-0871-2 (pbk.) — ISBN 978-1-4777-0872-9 (6-pack)
  1. Greece—Civilization—To 146 B.C.–Juvenile literature. I. Title.
  DF77.B527 2014
  938—dc23
                                                    2012047887

Manufactured in the United States of America

CPSIA Compliance Information: Batch #S13PK2: For Further Information contact Rosen Publishing, New York, New York at 1-800-237-9932

CONTENTS

Ancient Greek Culture

The people who made up the ancient Greek **civilization** lived in Greece a very long time ago. When **historians** talk about ancient Greece, they are generally talking about the civilization that existed in the years between about 750 BC and around AD 500.

Ancient Greece is famous for its rich **culture**. What does culture mean, though? Culture is a word used to talk about a civilization's rules for living and working together and its beliefs, values, customs, arts, and **technology**. American culture has been around for only a few hundred years, while ancient Greek culture spanned over 1,300 years. Are you ready to find out more about it?

Many historians believe that ancient Greek culture was the basis for modern Western culture. The ancient Greeks were known for many things, including their beautiful architecture, or the designs of their buildings and temples.

Greek Mythology

One of the biggest parts of ancient Greek culture was its **religion**. Ancient Greeks believed in 12 main gods and goddesses, called the Olympians, as well as other minor gods. These gods and goddesses controlled everything in Greek life. Zeus, the god of the heavens, was the ruler of all the gods.

Athena was the Greek goddess of war and wisdom. She was also the patron goddess of Athens.

Zeus was the god of the sky and thunder. He took over the heavens by killing his father, who had eaten Zeus and his brothers and sisters to keep one of them from overthrowing him.

These gods were the main players in stories called **myths**. These myths explained the nature of things and how the world was created. Some myths gave rules for correct behavior, too. Can you think of any stories in our own culture that are like the myths of ancient Greece?

Temples

Zeus's temple was built in Olympia, which was the most sacred place in Greece and the place where the first Olympic Games took place.

The gods were so important to the ancient Greeks that they built many temples for them. Sometimes they used old buildings, such as forts, as temples, too. The temples were meant to serve as houses for the gods. People could visit the temple and say prayers or leave gifts for the gods.

Greek temples are generally broken into groups, called orders. These orders are based on the style of their columns. The orders are Doric, Ionic, and Corinthian. Doric columns were plain. Ionic columns had scroll designs at the top. Corinthian columns had flowers and leaves carved into the top.

Apollo, the god of light and the Sun, truth, healing, and music, had a well-known temple at Delphi, shown here.

The Acropolis and the Parthenon

One of the most famous places in ancient Greece was the Acropolis. The Acropolis was a fort set high on a hill above Athens. In fact, "acropolis" means "the highest place in the city." It had many buildings within its walls. One of the most well-known of these buildings is the Parthenon.

The Parthenon was built as a temple to Athena, the goddess of war and wisdom. Work on the temple started in 447 BC, and it was finally finished in 432. The Parthenon was built in the Doric style. It also had many beautiful **sculptures** and **friezes**.

The Parthenon is considered a symbol of the many achievements of the ancient Greek civilization. The Greek government is restoring the temple to make sure it is there for many years to come.

Religious Wisdom

The people of ancient Greece went to temples to make offerings. When they wanted advice on some problem, they went to an **oracle**. Oracles were the people through whom the gods and goddesses spoke. The answers people received from the oracles were also called oracles.

The most well-known oracle was found at Delphi, which stood on Mount Parnassus. People would travel great distances to ask questions of the Pythia there. The Pythia was the priestess at the temple of Apollo at Delphi. Apollo was the god of the Sun, truth, and music.

This is all that remains of the temple at Delphi. Some people feel the oracle's visions were caused by gases coming up from cracks in the earth of the temple.

Music and Dance

Music and dance were important parts of ancient Greek culture. Scientists have found parts of written songs and old instruments that tell them about music in this culture. There are also many paintings on urns from ancient Greece that show musicians playing and dancing during religious **rituals**, at weddings and funerals, and at banquets.

The Greeks believed there were nine Muses, goddesses who inspired Greek artists and musicians. Here one of the Muses is shown playing a lyre.

Much of what we know about Greek music and dance comes from scenes such as this one painted on the side of an urn from ancient Greece. An urn is a kind of vase or pot.

The Greeks played many instruments, but there were three main ones that were widely used. The lyre and the kithara were common stringed instruments. The aulos was a double-reed instrument. Reed instruments are those like the clarinet. The Greeks also sang as they played or danced.

Epic Poetry

In the *Odyssey*, Homer mentions the story of the Greeks ending a long siege on the city of Troy. They did it by building a huge horse and offered it as a gift to the city. The horse hid a force of soldiers inside.

Nearly every society has tried to pass on its history, myths, and legends. Ancient Greeks did this, too. One way they tried to do this was through epic poetry. Epic poems are very long poems that talk about the deeds of heroes. They were generally spoken out loud.

Two of the most famous epic poems were the *Iliad* and the *Odyssey*. A blind Greek named Homer is believed to have told these stories to people some 3,000 years ago. Though the stories are not completely true, they talk about the history of ancient Greece. The *Iliad* tells the story of a hero named Achilles and his battles against King Agamemnon during the last days of the Trojan War. The *Odyssey* tells about the travels of a hero named Odysseus as he heads home after the Trojan War ends.

This is the funeral mask of King Agamemnon, who was featured in the *Iliad*.

Theater and Drama

Theater and drama were important parts of ancient Greek culture. The ancient Greeks put on plays during religious festivals in honor of the god Dionysus. There were three main kinds of plays that the Greeks performed. One kind of play was called a comedy. Comedies generally made fun of the issues and people of the day.

Greek theaters were round, with benches surrounding the stage at the bottom. Sometimes up to 14,000 people would attend a play.

The priest of Dionysus had a special seat in the theater. Here he would have sat in the lion-footed seat, while other important officials would have sat in the other, plainer seats.

Tragedies were another kind of play. These plays generally talked about myths and legends of the past and were more serious than comedies. Satyr plays were focused on the kind of wild living related to Dionysus. A **chorus** of actors performed the plays.

Sculpture

Much of what we know about ancient Greek culture, history, and beliefs comes from the sculptures that were left behind. Greek sculptors were known for trying to sculpt the **ideal** human form. They often sculpted bronze or marble statues of the gods and goddesses or the heroes talked about in myths.

One kind of Greek sculpture is called a frieze. In this kind of sculpture, the sculptor carves a figure or a scene on a flat panel of stone.

Phidias is one of the best-known and greatest of the Greek sculptors. He worked on the Parthenon. His most famous sculptures were a huge statue of Zeus at Olympia and a statue of Athena at the Parthenon. He also carved many friezes around the Parthenon.

This is a bronze sculpture of Alexander the Great found in Egypt. Many bronze statues did not survive because the Greeks would melt them to get metal for weapons during wars.

Great Thinkers

Ancient Greece is perhaps best known for its many great **philosophers**, such as Socrates, Aristotle, and Plato.

Socrates taught his students by asking questions. He wanted them to learn to think for themselves. Plato spent a lot of time studying **politics**. He also founded the first university, called the Academy, in 387 BC. Aristotle thought people should learn about the world through hands-on experience and **observation**. Much of ancient Greek culture has influenced our own civilization. Thank you, ancient Greece.

Aristotle studied and wrote about a great number of topics. He was interested in the study of the way people think, animals, politics, theater, poetry, and the study of right and wrong.

GLOSSARY

chorus (KOR-us) A group of performers in Greek drama who sang or spoke as a group to highlight certain parts of the play.

civilization (sih-vih-lih-ZAY-shun) People living in a certain way.

culture (KUL-chur) The beliefs, practices, and arts of a group of people.

friezes (FREEZ-ez) Long, flat panels that have been carved or painted.

historians (hih-STOR-ee-unz) People who study the past.

ideal (eye-DEEL) Describing something that is just right.

myths (MITHS) Stories that people make up to explain events.

observation (ahb-ser-VAY-shun) Something that is seen or noticed.

oracle (AWR-uh-kul) A person who was supposedly able to know things that had not happened yet.

philosophers (fih-LAH-suh-ferz) People who try to discover and to understand the basic nature of knowledge.

politics (PAH-lih-tiks) The science of governments and elections.

religion (rih-LIH-jen) A belief in and a way of honoring a god or gods.

rituals (RIH-choo-ulz) Special series of actions done for reasons of faith.

sculptures (SKULP-cherz) Figures that are carved or formed.

technology (tek-NAH-luh-jee) The way that people do something using tools and the tools that they use.

INDEX

WEBSITES

Due to the changing nature of Internet links, PowerKids Press has developed an online list of websites related to the subject of this book. This site is updated regularly. Please use this link to access the list:
www.powerkidslinks.com/sacg/cult/